Are you ready for
awesome virtual travel
around the world?

Stunning Beauty!

Awesome Pictures of Famous Places in the World Photography for Kids

Children's Arts, Music & Photography Books

All Rights reserved. No part of this book may be reproduced or used in any way or form or by any means whether electronic or mechanical, this means that you cannot record or photocopy any material ideas or tips that are provided in this book

Copyright 2016

Ayers Rock can be found in Australia. The rock can change its color during the day depending on the Sun.

Sydney Opera House is located in Sydney Australia. It is one of the famous live music venues.

Angkor Wat is Cambodias most famous tourist destination. It is the largest religious monument in the world.

The Great Wall of China is the longest man made structure. The Great Wall of China is around 3915 miles long.

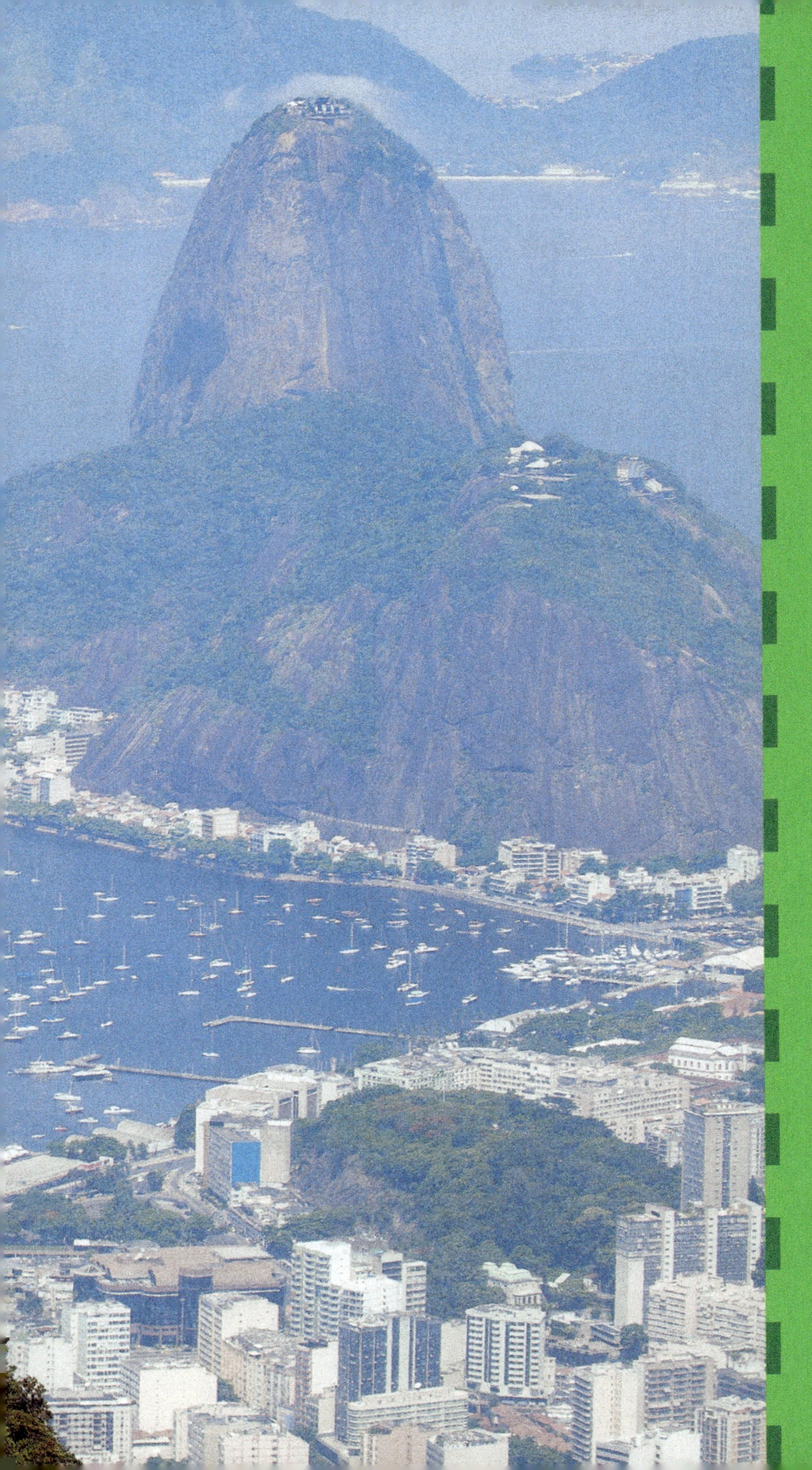

Christ the Redeemer is a symbol of Brazilian Christianity. It is one of the New Seven Wonders of the World.

Niagara falls is located in the Border of Ontario Canada and New York, USA. 30 million tourists visit Niagara Falls every year.

The Great Sphinx was built more than 4000 years ago. They were built to guard tombs and temples.

The Great Pyramid of Giza is the largest Egyptian pyramid. It took 20 years to build the pyramid.

Stonehenge is one of the famous sites in the world. It is located in England.

The Acropolis of Athens is the remains of an ancient city in Greece. It was built as a fortress where the people could stay when the city was attacked.

The Taj Mahal is located in Agra, India. It took 20 years to complete the construction.

The Colosseum was built during the Roman empire. 50,000 people could fit in it.

The Machu Picchu was a city of Incas. It is located 7970 feet above sea level.

The Bryce Canyon is located in Utah. The canyon is named after Ebenezer Bryce, a Mormon pioneer.

The Golden Gate Bridge is one of the Seven Wonders of the Modern World. The length of the bridge is 8981 feet.

Angel falls is the highest waterfall in the world. The water drops from the height of 979 meters.

Victoria Falls is one of the world's largest waterfalls. It is located on the Zambezi River in Africa.

Do you want to travel and visit the famous places around the world?

CPSIA information can be obtained
at www.ICGtesting.com
Printed in the USA
BVOW05s0130151216
470886BV00005B/19/P